A Painful History of Childhood

Freaky Fashion
and
Foul Food

John Townsend

www.raintreepublishers.co.uk

Visit our website to find out more information about **Raintree** books.

To order:

 Phone 44 (0) 1865 888112

 Send a fax to 44 (0) 1865 314091

💻 Visit the Raintree Bookshop at www.raintreepublishers.co.uk to browse our catalogue and order online.

First published in Great Britain by
Raintree, Halley Court, Jordan Hill,
Oxford OX2 8EJ, part of Harcourt Education.
Raintree is a registered trademark of Harcourt
Education Ltd.

© Harcourt Education Ltd 2006
First published in paperback 2007
The moral right of the proprietor has
been asserted.

Editorial: Melanie Waldron and Lucy Beevor
Design: Philippa Jenkins and Q2A
Illustrations: Q2A
Picture Research: Mica Brancic and
Elaine Willis
Production: Chloe Bloom
Originated by Modern Age
Printed and bound in China by South China
Printing Company

10 digit ISBN 1 406 20076 X (hardback)
13 digit ISBN 978 1 406 20076 8

10 digit ISBN 1 406 20083 2 (paperback)
13 digit ISBN 978 1 406 20083 6

11 10 09 08 07
10 9 8 7 6 5 4 3 2 1

**British Library Cataloguing in
Publication Data**
Townsend, John
Freaky fashion and foul food. –
(A painful history of childhood)
391.3'09
A full catalogue record for this book is
available from the British Library.

Acknowledgements
Advertising Archives p. 23; AKG-Images pp. 10–11,
16; Bridgeman Art Library pp. 20–21, pp. 25
(Archives Charmet), 10 (Ashmolean Museum,
University of Oxford, UK), 12 (Johnny van Haeftn
Gallery, London, UK); British Library pp. 12–13;
Corbis pp. 18–19, 27, 38, pp. 40 (Becky Lulgart-
Stayner), 33 (Cardinale Stephane), 31 (Frans
Lanting), 14 (Galen Rowell), 6 (Gianni Dagli Orti),
35 (H. Armstrong Roberts), title and 17 (Hulton-
Deutsch Collection), 11 (J. Barry O'Rourke),
pp. 5(t), 8 (Janet Wishnetsky), 24 (Joel Bennett),
38–39 (Karen Mason Blair), 4 (Kevin Fleming), 13
(Kevin Schafer), 21 (Lois Ellen Frank), 9 (Michael
Freeman), 29 (Reuters/Lee Besford), 31 (Richard T.
Nowitz), 28–29 (Robert van der Hilst), 30 (Zuma/
Mike Valdez); Corbis/Bettmann pp. 34–35, 34, 36;
Eye Ubiquitous p. 28; Getty Images pp. 7 (Dorling
Kindersley/ Dave King), 22–23 (FoodPix/ Paul
Poplis), 43 (Hulton Archive), 42 (Matthew Peyton),
8–9 (Stone/ Yann Layma), 5(b) and 37 (Taxi), 43
(Time & Life Pictures); Kobal pp. 24–25, 39; Mary
Evans Picture Library pp. 14–15, 17, 19, 20;
PYMCA/ ©Jason Manning pp. 4–5; Rex Features
pp. 5(m), 26–27, and 32 33 (Csaba Segesvari), 26
(Guy Call), 41 (Peter Brooker), 40–41 (Peter De
Voecht), 37 (Stills Press Agency); The Art
Archive/Dagli Orti p. 6.

Cover photograph of two female models wearing hats,
reproduced with permission of Alamy/V & A Images.

The publishers would like to thank Bill Marriott
for his assistance in the preparation of this book.

Every effort has been made to contact copyright
holders of any material reproduced in this book.
Any omissions will be rectified in subsequent
printings if notice is given to the publishers.

The paper used to print this book comes from
sustainable resources.

Contents

Any words appearing in the text in bold, **like this**, are explained in the glossary. You can also look out for them in the Word bank at the bottom of each page.

Do adults know best?

For centuries, babies and children were thought of as "mini-adults", and were dressed in exactly the same clothes and given the same food as grown-ups. It is only recently that children are seen as having their own particular needs and tastes.

Few young children can eat and wear exactly what they like every day. Adults often decide for them. But as they grow older, most young people make it very clear what they like and what they hate. They certainly do not think that adults know best!

The past

Not so long ago, children and teenagers had very little say about what they ate or wore. If they did not like what they were given, they usually had to go without. All through history young people often had to put up with wearing and eating strange things. For some people the freaky fashion and foul food made childhood nasty, painful, or just plain embarrassing!

Many young people **rebel** against their parents by wearing their own choice of clothes, hairstyles, and jewellery.

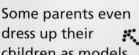

Some parents even dress up their children as models.

rebel   show anger or a strong dislike of authority

No choice

Growing bodies need the right food and clothing to keep them healthy. So why have adults sometimes fed unhealthy food to their children? Why have they let them dress in rags? Often parents had little choice or money, and had to use what was available at the time. Even today, millions of parents cannot afford to feed or clothe their children.

However freaky or foul some children's fashions and food from the past may seem now, they were still better than none at all.

Find out later

Why were Chinese girls' feet wrapped up to hurt so much?

What are the sickening secrets of the sausage?

How have the tastes of teens changed in the last 50 years?

Early times

Thousands of years ago children were treated very differently from the way they are treated today. They would have to accept whatever they were given to eat. They would also have to wear the style of clothes that their own **culture**, tribe, or **religion** demanded. These ways of dressing may seem odd or even funny to us today.

Ancient Egypt

Around 4,000 years ago Egyptian children had a distinct hairstyle. Both boys and girls wore a "side lock of youth". This was a **braided** lock of hair on the right side of their head. The rest of the head was shaved. Most of the time children wore no clothes, but teenagers wore white **tunics** like their parents.

King Tutankhamen died in his late teens in 1323 BC.

Royal children

The children of the Egyptian **pharaohs** dressed in fine clothes. Their robes and shirts were made of **linen**, which is light and cool. There were over 30 shirts found in the tomb of the young pharaoh Tutankhamen.

A young Egyptian boy wears his hair in a "side lock of youth".

Word bank   **braided**   strands of hair woven together
culture   behaviours, practices, and beliefs of a community

Egyptian food

The Egyptians grew wheat and barley on the fertile land beside the River Nile. At most meals families sat down to eat bread and beer – even for breakfast. Children grew up on this diet. However, it was terrible for their teeth. Sand and flakes of stone often got into the bread flour. When children chewed on the gritty bread their teeth soon wore down – sometimes to the roots.

The Egyptian cure for toothache was even worse. It involved putting a dead mouse on to the sore tooth, and sometimes even eating the mouse!

The ancient Egyptians also thought a dead, rotten mouse cured earache.

Did you know?

The Egyptians ate mice to cure a number of illnesses. A mouse roasted to a cinder and ground into a basin of milk was said to be a cure for a child's cough. A mouse cooked in oil was used to stop hair turning grey. Do you think these treatments actually worked?

pharaoh   ruler of ancient Egypt
tunic   knee-length robe worn by ancient Egyptians, Greeks, and Romans

Ancient China

For nearly 1,000 years in China it was fashionable for girls to have tiny feet. Their shoes had to be as small as possible, because tiny feet were seen as dainty and high class. It became the **custom** to bind up girls' feet with tight strips of cloth to stop them growing properly. Many girls had to go through great pain for this fashion.

Between the ages of three to six, girls had their feet bound up. The bindings were taken off each day and then rewound even tighter. It would hurt so much that they would often scream. Sometimes the girls' toes would be broken and folded right under the foot.

A story tells of a Chinese prince 3,000 years ago who loved to see women with tiny feet dance. Their dainty feet became a sign of great beauty and style. He made his young dancers tie their feet in tight bandages to stop them growing. Soon all girls had to suffer this painful foot-binding.

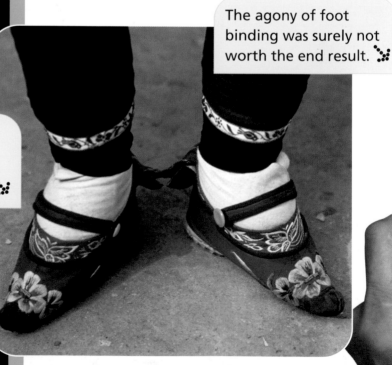

The agony of foot binding was surely not worth the end result.

Small feet were a sign of great beauty in ancient China.

Word bank   **custom**   usual way of doing things over a long period of time

More pain

Often the girls' bound toes lost all feeling when the blood supply became cut off. This led to **gangrene**, where the toes turned black and sometimes fell off. Some girls were never able to stand again. Others could not walk or stand without a great deal of pain.

After two or three years of binding, the feet were **deformed** enough to be squeezed into tiny shoes just 8 centimetres (3.1 inches) long. The special shoes were made of silk and covered with beautiful patterns. They were the height of fashion. Many Chinese women envied those with such tiny feet, and they tried to squeeze their own feet into the tiny shoes. Foot binding was finally banned in 1911.

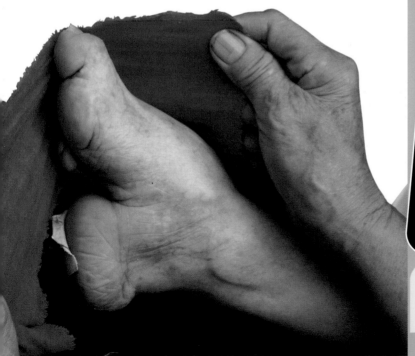

A white bird's nest is collected to make bird's nest soup.

gangrene when flesh dies and rots due to lack of blood supply

9

Roman babies were given a special necklace called a *bulla*. It was thought to protect children against evil. Boys wore their *bulla* until they were sixteen. Afterwards it was only worn on special occasions. A girl wore her bulla until her wedding. Then it was put away with her toys.

An original Roman *bulla*, dating from AD 100

Romans

The Romans were proud of their strong armies. It was important for soldiers to look smart to gain everyone's respect. Young Romans also had to look smart if they were to become good Roman citizens.

Young wealthy people in Rome wore knee-length **tunics**. A boy's tunic was white with a crimson edge. When he reached sixteen years old, he was called a man. He could then wear a plain white tunic called a **toga**. Girls' tunics were belted at the waist. When they went outside, girls wore long tunics that reached down to the ground.

Word bank   **toga**   loose outer garment worn by citizens of ancient Rome

Big food

Lower-class Romans and their young slaves ate bread, often dipped in wine – and that was just for breakfast! Richer children would often buy food, such as pancakes with raisins on top, from bakeries on their way to school.

Children who lived in rich households would often join their parents at huge **banquets**. These massive feasts had piles of rich food that people gorged themselves on.

Did you know?

Very rich Romans, such as the Emperor Nero, sent slaves up to the mountains to fetch snow. The snow was then made into a sort of ice cream, and mixed with fruit and honey. You could say that the Romans invented the "slush-puppy!"

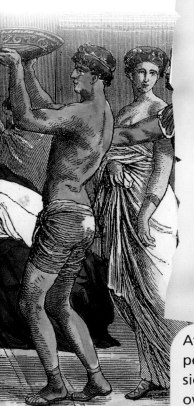

BANQUET MENU

STARTER
PEACOCK TONGUES
FOLLOWED BY ROAST PUPPY

MAIN COURSE
CHICKEN STUFFED INSIDE
DUCK, WITH THE DUCK
INSIDE GOOSE, THE GOOSE
INSIDE PIG, AND THE PIG
INSIDE COW

DESSERT
STUFFED DATES, SALTED,
AND FRIED IN HONEY

At some Roman banquets people ate until they were sick, and then started all over again!

Today's ice cream is very different from the snow and fruit of Roman times.

The years from about AD 600 to 1500 are now called the Middle Ages, or sometimes Medieval Times. It was tough growing up in those days. Young people's food and fashion was usually the same as everyone else's – dull, dirty, and **dismal**.

Middle Ages

A thousand years ago, most families across Europe struggled to feed and clothe their children. Parents often had more babies in those days to replace children they had lost to hunger or disease.

If a baby survived being born, it was washed in warm water and then wrapped in cotton or wool. After that, children and their clothes were unlikely to get washed again!

Peasants burned logs to warm their homes and cook their food, so people's clothes would smell of the wood smoke. At least that hid their body smells! Young people dressed the same as their parents, usually in drab browns and greys. Only the rich could afford to wear bright fine silks.

Servants wait on a Medieval family at a banquet around 1323.

A huge pan of soup boils over the fire in a Medieval home.

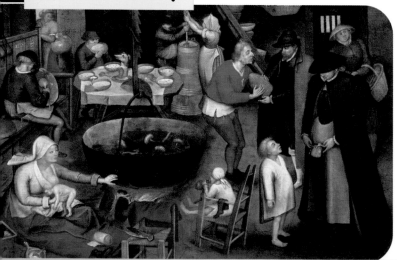

Word bank   **protein** important part of the human diet, in foods like meat, milk, and eggs

Dull food

Peasant children in the **Middle Ages** would not have had much choice in what they ate. Nearly every meal would have been a thick, brown soup called **pottage**. This was barley porridge mixed with boiled onions, cabbage, and any other plants that could be eaten.

People in the Middle Ages did not eat many raw vegetables, so children were often ill from not having enough **vitamins** in their food. The lucky ones could sometimes add a few scraps of salted pork or fatty bacon to their pottage, which would add flavour and **protein**. Protein is very important for helping bodies to grow.

Gross grub

Rich families in the Middle Ages ate well. Huge **banquets** were full of different types of meat, from larks and geese, to eels and salmon. If that was not enough to satisfy hungry stomachs, there was mashed deer tongues served on fried bread. If people were still not full, they could finish with deer-antler soup or puffin cooked and soaked in vinegar.

Salted or smoked puffin is still eaten in parts of Iceland.

vitamins   important chemicals needed in small amounts in our food to keep us healthy

Foul fabrics & ghastly garments

At different times and in different countries, parents have wrapped up children and babies in the most uncomfortable clothes.

Looking cool, keeping warm

The way young people dressed in the past usually depended on the weather – just like today. People growing up in the jungle under a blazing sun wear very little, if anything at all. But people living in very cold places have more important things to worry about than the latest fashion. Clothes made from **caribou** fur or sealskin are the only clothes warm enough for living in such cold climates. Looking strange does not matter when you have to survive freezing cold temperatures!

Dressed in seal skin

Inuit people (above) still wear special clothes for keeping out the bitterly cold wind. Kamiks are waterproof leg-warmers. The feet are made of sealskin, and the rest is made of seal fur. The patterns on kamiks are different for boys and girls. Girls' kamiks have bead work on the top of the foot, making them very stylish.

Word bank   **caribou** large North American reindeer, with large antlers

Freaky heads

The Dayak people of Borneo used to believe that a flat forehead was a sign of great beauty. They wrapped their babies up tightly to stop them moving, and then placed weights on their head to flatten the forehead. Some tribes in Africa also changed the shape of their babies' heads by tightly wrapping and stretching them.

In some parts of Europe, such as Normandy in France, head stretching was done until the late 1800s. Babies' heads were wrapped in tight bandages, which were left on for months. The pressed skull gave them a flat head, which was the height of fashion.

Strong backs

Native American babies were carried around on pieces of wood, called cradle boards. Their parents felt this would give their children a strong back and nicely rounded head.

The Dayak people believed that a child with a flat forehead was clever and closer to the spirit world.

Wrapping up babies

Many babies in the **Middle Ages** in Europe were bound tightly in **swaddling** clothes. The babies were tied up in **linen** strips, like an Egyptian mummy. This kept them warm and stopped them wriggling around. In the 1500s babies would have their cloth nappies changed about once a week – if they were lucky. The nappies were tied on with string, as safety pins were not invented until 1849.

Inuit native people of northern North America and eastern Siberia who live in the Arctic

Ancient Egyptians and Romans wore **loincloths** under their **tunics**, but where did the word "underpants" actually come from? The answer is from pantaloons – a French fashion item for men in the 1600s. Pantaloons were close-fitting trousers, like tights. They were often worn with straps under the feet to hold them tightly in place.

Underwear

Hardly anyone wore underwear in Europe in the **Middle Ages**. Even though underpants were invented in the 1200s, poor people went without them for hundreds of years. Even if people did wear underwear, they did not wash or change it for weeks. Itchy, scratchy pants full of lice were probably worse than none at all!

New names

By the 1800s, more people were wearing underwear. Boys began wearing woollen knee-length underpants with a drawstring at the waist. These soon became known as drawers. Long, skin-tight underpants called "Long Johns" were first issued to US soldiers during World War 2 in the 1940s.

A 17th-century man wears pantaloons with a long cape. ✂

Word bank   **corset**   tight, stiff undergarment worn to give support or shape to the waist and hips

The painful history of corsets

Teenage girls had to suffer if they were to become beautiful ladies. Although rich women had worn **corsets** for hundreds of years, many people by the 1830s thought all girls needed them to keep their bodies in shape. Even four-year-old girls were laced up into tight canvas corsets. Teenage girls were strapped into heavier whalebone corsets to make their waists slimmer. The tight corsets could pull in their waists to a tiny 40 centimetres (16 inches). Some girls could hardly breathe and would keep fainting. Some even had to wear a corset at night, with their hands tied to stop them untying the garment.

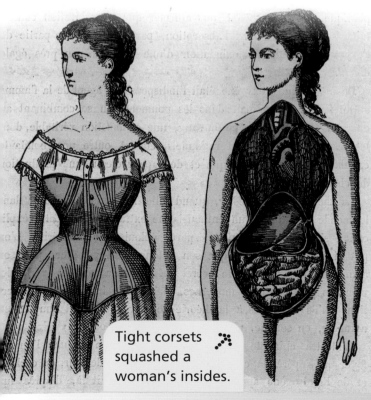

Tight corsets squashed a woman's insides.

nylon strong fabric made from chemicals

Many poorer mothers in cold countries used to sew children into their clothes during the winter. Layers of clothes would be sewn together to keep the child warm. Sometimes mothers would spread goose grease on to the child's skin first to add an extra-warm layer. The children would be "sewn-up" for months until the weather started to get warm again.

Fancy frocks

In the 1700s and 1800s, the children of rich families in Europe and the United States were dressed in the finest materials. Both young girls and boys were dressed in frilly and silky dresses. Parents liked their sons and daughters to look alike, so they dressed them both in **petticoats!**

Even teenage boys, who often wore **breeches** and waistcoats, had to wear shirts frilled with lace. In the late 1800s boys in the British royal family were dressed in blue and white sailor suits or **smocks**. This became the new fashion. Soon many boys across Europe and the United States were dressed like little sailors.

Word bank   **breeches**   short trousers that fit snugly at or just below the knee

Girls in trousers

In the 1900s, long after boys stopped wearing dresses, a few girls started to wear trousers. At first, the thought of females in trousers was very shocking to most people. But ideas about women's clothing began to change. Women were not expected to do much work outside the home, or take part in sports. But, during World Wars 1 and 2, many women worked in factories and on farms, as most men were away fighting. Skirts and dresses were not practical for this work, so more women started wearing trousers. By the 1960s, it was normal for teenage girls to wear trousers.

Even former US presidents were dressed up like little sailors! This is Franklin D. Roosevelt (standing between his grandparents) in 1890.

Boys in dresses

Can you believe that boys once had to wear dresses like the one pictured above in 1860? This dress is made from silk, with a pleated skirt, white collar, and ribbon trim. Parents probably liked this type of outfit much more than the children did!

petticoat   skirt or slip worn under a dress or outer skirt
smock   light, loose garment often worn over other clothes

Changing times

The Iroquois

For hundreds of years, Iroquois tribesmen hunted deer in what is now New York state. Boys were allowed to join in with the men after they had killed a deer by themselves. Girls helped to grow foods, such as beans and corn.

The first Europeans settled in North America in the 1600s. What they wore and ate slowly began to change as they **adapted** to their new surroundings. Some of them came into contact with Native Americans and saw how they fed and clothed their children.

Early America

The first **Pilgrims** lived in Massachusetts where the Wampanoag, a Native American tribe, also lived. The Wampanoag wore animal skins and feathers in their hair, which must have amazed the settlers. But the Wampanoag must also have been amazed at the clothes the first Pilgrims and their children wore.

The Iroquois tribesmen wore brightly-coloured feather headresses called *kostaweh*.

Many Europeans who settled in North America in the 1600s survived by learning from the Native American tribes.

Word bank adapt change to fit into a new situation
garters   band worn around the leg to hold up a stocking or soc

Different clothes

A Pilgrim boy would have worn stockings with **garters** to hold them up, **breeches**, and a felt hat. A Pilgrim girl would have dressed in a **petticoat**, stockings with garters, an apron, a waistcoat, and a close-fitting hat called a coif.

The Native Americans must also have been puzzled by the food of the settlers. Pilgrims ate bread, eggs, and milk from goats, while the Wampanoag would have eaten corn, beans, pumpkins, and meat. Before long, the Pilgrims began to eat many of the same foods as their way of life began to change.

Turkey and pumpkin pie are typical Thanksgiving foods.

Pilgrims   early European settlers in North America

Baked beans are older than you might think! When the **Pilgrims** arrived in North America, they learnt how to make baked beans from Native Americans. First, dried beans were baked in bear's fat. Next, pits were dug in the ground and lined with hot stones. Finally, the beans were covered in maple syrup and put on top of deerskin to bake slowly in the pit.

The new settlers added salt and pork to baked beans to make a dish called Boston Baked Beans. In the 1700s beans were served every Saturday night in New England. Sundays were spent in church, and no cooking was allowed on this **holy** day. Beans were left in the oven from the night before – keeping warm for when the family returned from church.

You can still find recipes for Boston Baked Beans in cookbooks today. ⚫⚫⚫

Word bank   **holy** set apart for worship

Full of beans

Before long, baked beans were feeding millions of people in the United States. Cowboys boiled up their beans on campfires. People began to add tomato sauce and, by 1895, flavoured baked beans were sold in cans by a businessman called Henry Heinz. The first cans of Heinz Baked Beans were made in the United Kingdom in 1928, where they quickly became a very popular new food.

Since the 1920s in the United States, the name Boston Baked Beans has been used to describe sweet, sugar-coated peanuts, which are nothing like the original dish.

Cold baked bean sandwich

In 1909 this recipe appeared in a US cookery book:

1) Butter two slices of Boston brown bread.

2) On one of these, spread a teaspoon of salad dressing. Add cold baked beans and a lettuce leaf.

3) Finish with the second slice of bread, a tablespoon of beans, cauliflower, and a teaspoon of dressing.

Baked beans are still going strong 400 years after they were first discovered.

Slops and sops

In poorer homes in the 1700s and 1800s, young children were fed the same food as their parents, but mashed up into a sloppy mush. They also ate a dish called sop, which was bread soaked in **broth**. The word "soup" came from this type of food.

Grey food

In the 1800s, cities around the world had **slums** where poor people lived. Children were always hungry and they would have been grateful for whatever food they were given. Babies, children, and adults ate the same food day in, day out. This was usually oats boiled in water or sometimes milk, to make porridge. Thinner, more watery porridge was called **gruel**. It was like a thin soup made by boiling any cereal in a pot of water. It was very dull. Sometimes gruel was flavoured with butter and pepper. Adding dried fruit or wine sauce on special occasions made it taste and look better.

A bowl of Mongolian stew made from sheep entrails. Do you think this would be tastier than gruel?

broth   liquid in which food has been cooked
gruel   watery soup made from mashed oats and scraps

Feeding the baby

Baby food was always made at home, and was often grey gruel or mashed-up scraps left from stewed bones and vegetables. It certainly was not full of the goodness that growing babies needed.

By the mid-1800s, food experts began to see the need for **mass-produced** food made just for babies. Food companies began to sell bottles and tins of milk-based baby food mixed with fruit and vegetables. They claimed this food would give babies a healthy, balanced diet. Canned baby food became big business in the 1900s.

In the movie *Oliver Twist*, Oliver famously requests more gruel, saying: "Please, sir. I want some more!"

Glass baby-bottles, made in France in the 1700s.

Baby bottles

Today babies are likely to be given milk from a plastic bottle. Thousands of years ago, mothers would use containers made from sheep's **udders**. Mothers in ancient Greece gave babies mixtures of wine and honey from china pots. Wood, leather, cow horns, and eventually glass were used in Europe to make feeding bottles for babies.

mass produced   many items made at once, all exactly the same

S-s-s-s-sausages

For hundreds of years poor people have eaten **offal**. This is made of the bits of dead animals left over after the meat is removed. The word offal comes from "off" and "fall" – meaning the pieces that fall from an animal **carcass**. This could be the heart, liver, lungs, tail, feet, or even the head. If that seems foul, you may actually have eaten some yourself. After all, this is what some sausages are made of!

Sausages have been eaten for over 2,000 years. The word sausage came from the Latin word *salsus*, which means something salted. Many years ago sausages were smothered with salt as this stopped the offal from going off.

Just what goes into a hot dog? In the past, it could have been anything!

Seven pigs went into this record-breaking 133 metre-(436 foot-) long sausage in Hungary, 2004.

Word bank   carcass   body of a dead animal
gristle   tough chewy meat, full of stringy tendons and fat

Hot dogs and burgers

Burgers and hot dogs have been popular ever since fast food first emerged in the United States in the early 1900s. But do people actually know what goes into these foods? Today there are strict rules about what sort of animal parts can be used to make sausages and burgers.

If burgers are made from beef, why are they called hamburgers? There are many ideas about this. One is that German people from the city of Hamburg, who went to live in the United States in the 1880s, introduced sandwiches with ground beef inside them. These became known as "Hamburger steaks".

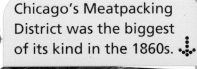
Chicago's Meatpacking District was the biggest of its kind in the 1860s.

Shocking sausages

Around the early 1900s the writer Upton Sinclair visited the Meatpacking District of Chicago, United States. What he wrote after his visit shocked people. He told how dead rats were thrown into sausage-grinding machines, and diseased cows were made into beefburgers. Laws were soon made to stop this happening.

offal   organs and other parts trimmed from an animal that has been killed for food

Food & fashion extremes

Many **cultures** around the world have extreme ways of decorating their bodies. Some of these decorations seem very unpleasant to people outside of these cultures.

Brass necks and piercings

The Paduang tribe in Thailand are part of a hill tribe group called the Karen. The girls in the tribe have heavy, brass rings fitted around their necks from the age of five or six. Several rings are added each year, and the collarbone and ribs are slowly pushed down giving the impression of a stretched neck. This ancient fashion is **unique** to the Paduang, and they are often nicknamed the "Long Neck" tribe because of it.

Growing pains

Marking the body in some way to show that a child has become an adult is a part of many cultures. Among the Guarani people of Brazil, boys have a thin, hardened stick pushed through their nose or upper lip (below) to show that they have grown up.

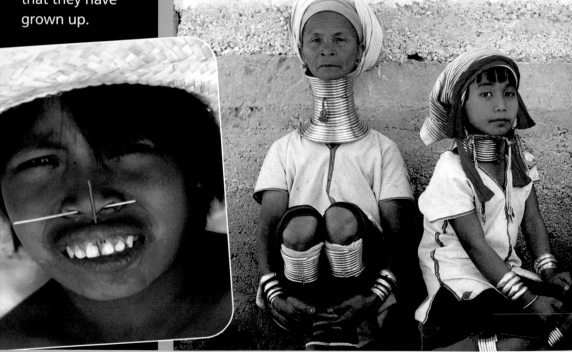

Word bank   **unique** unlike anything else

Holes in the body

Painful as it might seem, the fashion of piercing a hole through the skin and inserting a piece of metal, bone, shell, or glass as jewellery has been around for thousands of years. Sometimes the piercing is worn to show that a person belongs to a certain tribe or group.

Body piercing is still fashionable with men, women, and young people all around the world. Piercings can be decorated with rings, studs, and bars. They can appear in ears, navels, tongues, eyebrows, nostrils – in fact, just about anywhere on the body!

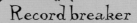

The women of the Paduang tribe can never remove the rings from their neck. After so long wearing them, the neck is no longer able to support itself.

A tattoo can be a real pain in the neck!

How do I look?

For many young people body piercing, daring clothes, and extreme hair styles can be a mark of **identity** or a way of **rebelling** against older people. Yet extreme body art for young people is nothing new. Over 10,000 years ago, young men and women used all kinds of body make-up to colour their skin and hair.

Fashion statement

A **tattoo** is made with a needle that punctures deep into the skin, injecting ink into the surface. The pattern that is made will last for life. Some people go through a lot of pain and risk of **infection** to get a tattoo, only to find that they no longer want it in later life.

Patterned bodies

In New Zealand some **Maori** men had painful tattoos called moko scratched over their faces. These were done using tiny **chisels**. The tattooing started when boys were in their teens, and carried on throughout their lives. In time, their whole bodies became covered with patterns. Women tattooed their lips and chins only. The tattooing was very painful, and often caused swellings to the skin. But the Maori considered people without tattoos to be naked. Over the last twenty years moko has become fashionable amongst young Maoris again.

Did you know?

Tattoos are nothing new. They have decorated people's skin for thousands of years. They have been found on ancient mummies in tombs in Egypt.

Word bank   chisel   metal tool with a cutting edge for chipping away solid material

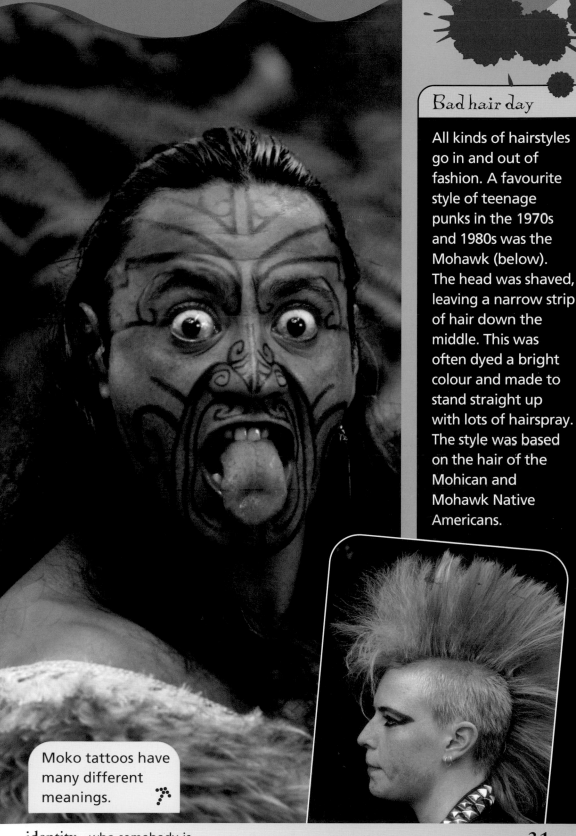

All kinds of hairstyles go in and out of fashion. A favourite style of teenage punks in the 1970s and 1980s was the Mohawk (below). The head was shaved, leaving a narrow strip of hair down the middle. This was often dyed a bright colour and made to stand straight up with lots of hairspray. The style was based on the hair of the Mohican and Mohawk Native Americans.

Moko tattoos have many different meanings.

identity who somebody is
Maori native people of New Zealand

Snacks from the wild

Some **cultures** around the world eat things you might not normally think of as food. Insects and their **larvae** provide high levels of **nutrients**, and they can be eaten raw, fried, or roasted. They probably also taste good!

- In parts of Africa people have eaten **locusts** for thousands of years.
- **Maoris** in New Zealand eat the huhu bug, which is a type of beetle.
- In Nigeria, Africa, children are fed roast termites and crickets.

Ancient insect dishes

The ancient Romans and Greeks ate lots of insects. Rich Romans loved to eat beetle larvae that had been fed on flour and wine.

Aristotle, a Greek writer in the 4th century BC, wrote:

"THE LARVA OF THE **CICADA** TASTES BEST. THE MALES ARE GOOD TO EAT, BUT THE FEMALES ARE FULL OF WHITE EGGS."

Could you bring •••⟩ yourself to eat a live witchetty grub?

Word bank

| cicada | insect related to leafhoppers |
| larvae | grubs that hatch from the eggs of insects |

Grub's up!

Aboriginal people from Australia eat many different kinds of insects. Long ago, some tribes would gather at the Bogong Mountains to eat Bogong moths, which were cooked in hot ashes. Some of the moths were ground into paste and made into cakes.

Another important insect for Aborigines was the witchetty grub. This is the plump larva of a moth. The grubs were eaten raw or cooked in ashes. The fat white grubs are high in **protein** and are said to taste like peanut butter. Children still love them even today. The grubs are often offered to tourists in parts of Australia.

A meal of worms

In the United States some restaurants are now putting insect dishes on the menu. Stir-fried mealworms and caterpillar crunch are served alongside a side order of chips. Chocolate covered grasshoppers are also a favourite. Some Japanese restaurants serve boiled wasp larvae, fried cicadas, fried grasshoppers, and fried silk moth larvae.

A selection of insect dishes, which are now being served in many restaurants across the United States and Japan.

locust large grasshopper that flies in huge swarms
nutrient chemical in food that the body needs to grow and stay healthy

33

Looking good, having fun

Dressed for school

For hundreds of years in the United States, children could only go to school if their parents could pay for them to attend. Such schools had their own special uniforms, and many private schools still do today.

Never before have young people in richer countries had such choice in what they can eat and wear. So does that make them happy? Not always! Many teenagers feel under pressure to wear the "right" clothes or designer labels. This can create a lot of stress.

Uniform

The pressures of having to wear the latest fashion can be eased if schools have their own uniform. Although most students in the United States can wear what they like, some schools have developed a **dress-code** or a set uniform. In the United Kingdom, it is more common for pupils to wear a school uniform until the age of sixteen.

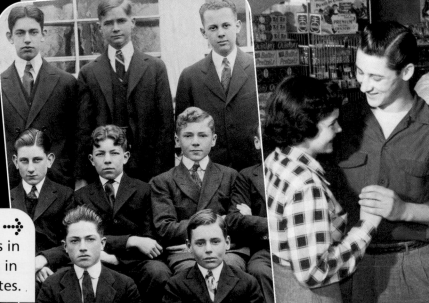

Children wore ⋯⟩ smart uniforms in private schools in the United States.

Word bank   **dress-code** dressing to certain rules and standards

Teenage fashions

Wearing the right labels and styles are important for many modern teenagers. Teenage fashion is big business today. But over 60 years ago, there was no such thing as teenage fashion. Things began to change in the 1940s.

Young people were first seen as a big fashion market in the United States during World War 2. Many teenagers took on jobs that were left behind by the men fighting as soldiers. They soon had lots of pocket money to spend on new clothes!

Seventeen Magazine started in 1944 and began to feature clothes and fashions aimed just at young people. Teenagers and their clothes started taking the world by storm.

"Cateye" glasses were shaped to look like cat's eyes, and were a favourite fashion item for girls in the 1950s.

Poodle skirts

US teenage girls in the 1950s just had to have a poodle skirt! A poodle skirt was a wide skirt with a poodle design on the fabric. These types of skirts have recently come back into fashion in European countries.

Teenagers wear the latest fashions in a US **soda fountain**, around 1947.

soda fountain   counter for serving drinks, sodas, sundaes, and ice cream

Elvis

The 1950s and 1960s saw the growth of a new music style called rock and roll. Many older people thought this music was far too noisy and they hated the Elvis Presley look that many teenagers copied. The Elvis haircut and tight drain pipe trousers became very trendy.

Fast food

Freaky fashions for young people really took off in the 1950s and 1960s. Not only did teenagers have their own styles of clothes, but they also had their own meeting places. They would gather for a milkshake or cola at **soda fountains** or drive-in diners. It was a "fab" (short for fabulous) time to be a teenager.

During the 1960s the idea of fast food really took off in the United States. Many of the new places to eat promised good family fun, speedy service, and low prices. They were also the perfect place for teenagers to hang out.

Everything about Elvis Presley excited teenagers in the 1950s. He became an instant fashion and music icon.

slogan   word or phrase used by a group to attract attention

Funky flares

At the start of the 1970s, trousers were gently flared at the bottom, but they soon became wide bell-bottoms. Many people wore huge platform shoes under their flares. Some platform shoes had soles that were so thick that people sometimes fell off their shoes and twisted their ankles. In fact, such fashion was nothing new. The ancient Romans wore platform shoes so they could walk through puddles without getting the bottom of their **togas** wet.

Punk was another teenage fashion of the late 1970s. Some punks wore clothes covered in safety pins, spikes, and painted **slogans**. Combined with spiky hair and punk music, many teens of the 1970s and 1980s used their image to **rebel** like never before.

Hairy times

Much to the disapproval of many older people, boys began to grow their hair long in the 1960s. The Beatles were the most famous pop group during the 1960s, and their "mop-top" hairstyle became fashionable around the world (below). Some people even wore wigs to recreate the famous look. Many girls also wore their hair like the Beatles.

Sparkling platform shoes were the height of fashion in the 1970s.

Cool feet

A boom in **aerobics** in the 1980s turned ordinary training clothes into designer fashion items. **Leotards**, sweatbands, and headbands were worn as everyday clothes. The prices for trainers shot up, and a few people were even mugged for their trendy trainers.

Labels to rebels

Designer wear for teens, toddlers, and even babies is big business in many countries today. Advertisements on television and in magazines tell us we that we should wear the right labels to be cool. Some young people feel huge pressure to keep buying all the right clothes to look a certain way.

In the 1980s designer clothes with labels became a way for young people to show they had style. Brand names became a sign of wealth and good taste. Designer labels spread to sportswear, perfume, bags, and luggage. People no longer wore jeans just for comfort – they had to be the right brand, with the label on full display.

Grunge

As the 1980s turned into the 1990s one fashion trend hit back at the designer label look. Some US rock bands started the trend of dressing down, which became known as Grunge. This was the complete opposite to the designer label look. Their clothes suggested that they were rejecting all the expensive clothes and possessions that had become fashionable in the 1980s.

Pop stars such as Cher, shown here in 1989, helped to make training clothes fashionable in the 1980s.

Word bank   aerobics   system of exercises to develop and tone the body

Grunge fashion and music began in Seattle, Washington, but quickly spread around the United States and the world. Ripped jeans, flannel shirts, Doctor Marten™ boots, or footwear called Converse™ canvas hi-tops became part of the 1990s' youth fashion statement.

Films and television have had a great effect on teen fashions over the years. In 1995 the film *Clueless* was the most popular teen comedy. The schoolgirl look of baby doll dresses with puffed sleeves and thigh-high socks became popular because of this film.

The 1995 film *Clueless* is a comedy about rich teenagers who can afford all the best clothes.

leotard   close-fitting, one-piece garment worn mostly by athletes and dancers

Growing tastes

Many young people are now brought up on spicy food from around the world. Tex-Mex is hot spicy food that came from the US state of Texas and Mexico in Central America. Tex-Mex food became widely popular from the 1970s. Even young children enjoy the hot spicy meat, beans, and tortilla chips.

Let's party

Today, there are millions of fast food outlets all over the world that cater for young peoples' tastes. Never before have people had such a wide choice of food to eat. But even some tasty food can still be "foul food". Eating too much of the wrong kinds of food is a major problem facing young people today.

The problem often starts with very young children. Many will only eat food that is brightly-coloured and looks fun. Things like deep-fried, fun-shapes of meat full of fat, salt, and colours look more exciting than green vegetables. However, now that many children are becoming **obese**, people have realised that healthy eating needs to be taught from an early age. This means cutting down on all the foods that are bad for us.

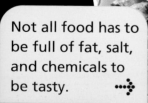

Not all food has to be full of fat, salt, and chemicals to be tasty.

Word bank   **epidemic**   major health problem that affects many people over a wide area

Unhealthy

Over the last 25 years young people have eaten more burgers, chicken nuggets, chips, hot dogs, doughnuts, and ice cream than ever before. They have also spent less time playing outside. The number of children who are overweight has doubled in that time. Almost half of US children aged eight to sixteen watch three to five hours of television a day. Many of them eat too much and move around too little. This is why doctors say child obesity is now an **epidemic** in the United States. It is the same in many other countries. The "foul food" of today might lead to tomorrow's major health problems.

Obesity can lead to serious health problems, such as heart disease and diabetes. At the very least, eating greasy food all the time can leave you feeling tired and unfit.

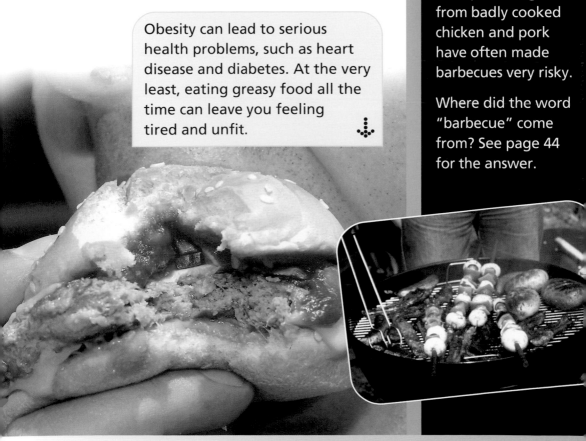

Barbecues

Cooking and eating outside at parties has become very popular over the last 30 years. Grilling meat on barbecues (below) and eating it with fingers is all good fun – but it is not always healthy eating. Burn accidents and food poisoning from badly cooked chicken and pork have often made barbecues very risky.

Where did the word "barbecue" come from? See page 44 for the answer.

obese   being overweight for your age and height

Designer toddlers

Many parents now feel the pressure of having to dress their babies and young children in the very latest fashions . . . at the latest high prices! The trouble is, the children soon grow and the parents have to buy bigger clothes. It can cost parents a lot of money.

Just be you!

Body image matters to many people today. It sometimes seems as if the **media** is sending out the message that successful people should look a certain way, wear particular hairstyles, and have the right body shape. Beautiful models, pop stars, and actors sometimes make us feel that we need to look just like them to have friends and be happy. However, it should not be our looks that make us feel happy, but how we feel inside.

It seems that even children must keep up with the latest fashions these days!

Word bank   **media**   newspapers, films, television, and the Internet

What next?

In the last 50 years, tastes in clothes and food have changed more quickly than ever before. Today, everyone wants the latest product or the newest fashion. Food and clothes companies now spend millions of pounds on advertising to get us to buy their new products.

Many young people are very lucky to have such a wide choice of clothes and food to keep them feeling healthy and looking good. Much of the freaky fashion and foul food from the past has long gone, but who can tell what scary things young people will be eating and wearing tomorrow?

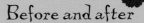

Even N*Sync, one of the most fashionable groups, got it wrong in 1990!

Designers in the 1960s predicted these "space-age" outfits would be the fashion of the future.

Find out more

Answer from page 41

Where did the word *barbecue* come from? Any of the following explanations could be true. Maybe it came from the French term *de barbe et queue*, or "from beard to tail" – meaning an animal is cooked whole. Or maybe barbecue came from the Taino people of the Caribbean. The Taino word *barabicu*, means "fire pit". Which do you think it could be?

Further reading

20th Century Fashion – the 80s and 90s, Clare Lomas (Heinemann Library, 2000)

Food & Feasts in the Middle Ages, Lynne Elliott (Crabtree, 2004)

The Fashionable History of Make-Up & Body Decoration, Helen Reynolds (Heinemann Library, 2003)

Using the Internet

Explore the Internet to find out more about childhood fashion and food. You can use a search engine, such as **www.yahooligans.com**, and type in keywords such as:

- flares
- pantaloons
- Thanksgiving food.

Search tips

There are billions of pages on the Internet so it can be difficult to find exactly what you are looking for.

These search tips will help you find useful websites more quickly:

- Know exactly what you want to find out about first.
- Use two to six keywords in a search, putting the most important words first.
- Be precise. Only use names of people, places, or things.

Could you stomach it?

These are just some of the freaky foods that have been added to restaurant menus in recent times:

MAGGOTS ON THE MENU

May 2005

A German restaurant claims to be fully booked for weeks after adding maggots to the menu. The restaurant in Dresden, Germany, has maggot ice cream, maggot salads, and maggot cocktails.

"We started serving them about a month ago as a bit of a joke but people come back again, and usually bring more friends with them," the owner said. Teenager Sarah Azubi, seventeen, said, "I had maggots deep-fried. They were crunchy like chips and tasted a bit like nuts, with a crunchy shell around a soft juicy bit in the middle."

"SNAIL PORRIDGE" CHEF'S TOP AWARD

April 2004

A restaurant serving dishes including snail porridge and smoked bacon-and-egg ice cream has been named the second best in the world.

The Fat Duck in Bray, Berkshire, United Kingdom, is second only to California's French Laundry, according to 300 judges.

Amongst other weird and wonderful dishes, Chef Heston Blumenthal serves up sardine-on-toast sorbet, beetroot jelly, and salmon poached with liquorice.

Glossary

Aborigine native people of Australia

adapt change to fit into a new situation

aerobics system of exercises to develop and tone the body

banquet a large feast for many people

braided strands of hair woven together

breeches short trousers fitting snugly at or just below the knee

broth liquid in which food has been cooked

carcass body of a dead animal

caribou large North American reindeer, with large antlers

chisel metal tool with a cutting edge for chipping away solid material

cicada insect related to leafhoppers

corset tight, stiff undergarment worn to give support or shape to the waist and hips

culture behaviour, practices, and beliefs of a community

custom usual way of doing things over a long period of time

deform spoil natural shape

dismal very gloomy and depressing

dress-code dressing to certain rules and standards

epidemic major health problem that affects many people over a wide area

gangrene when flesh dies and rots due to lack of blood supply

garters band worn round the leg to hold up a stocking or sock

gristle tough chewy meat, full of stringy tendons and fat

gruel watery soup made from mashed oats and stewed scraps

holy set apart for worship

identity who somebody is

infection poisoned or diseased part of the body

ingredient one part of a mixture

Inuit native people of northern North America and eastern Siberia, who live in the Arctic

larvae grubs that hatch from the eggs of insects

leotard close-fitting, one-piece garment worn mostly by athletes and dancers

linen smooth, strong cloth made from flax plants

locust large grasshopper that flies in huge swarms

loincloth cloth worn round the waist, covering the upper thighs

Maori native people of New Zealand

mass produced many items made at once, all exactly the same

media newspapers, films, television, and the Internet

Middle Ages period around AD 600 to 1500

nutrient chemical in food that the body needs to grow and stay healthy

nylon strong fabric made from chemicals

obese being overweight for your age and height

offal organs and other parts trimmed from an animal that has been killed for food

peasant poor person or farm worker

petticoat skirt or slip worn under a dress or outer skirt

pharaoh ruler of ancient Egypt

Pilgrims early European settlers in North America

pottage thick soup of vegetables and cereals

protein important part of the human diet, in foods like meat, milk, and eggs

rebel show anger or a strong dislike of authority

religion system of beliefs and faith that give meaning to life

slogan word or phrase used by a group to attract attention

slums crowded, run-down part of a town or city, with poor living conditions

smock light, loose garment often worn over other clothes

soda fountain counter for serving drinks, sodas, sundaes, and ice cream

swaddling narrow strips of cloth wrapped around a baby to stop them from moving around

tattoo pattern made on the skin by making holes on the surface and filling them with ink

toga loose outer garment worn by citizens of ancient Rome

tunic knee-length robe worn by ancient Egyptians, Greeks, and Romans

vitamins important chemicals needed in small amounts in our food to keep us healthy

udder bit that hangs underneath a cow and supplies milk

unique unlike anything else

Index